THIS COLORING BOOK BELONGS TO:

COPYRIGHT 2022 HANDMADE BY KAYLEE BOOKS
ILLUSTRATED BY HANDMADEBYKAYLEE
VISIT WWW.INSTAGRAM.COM/HANDMADEBYKAYLEE

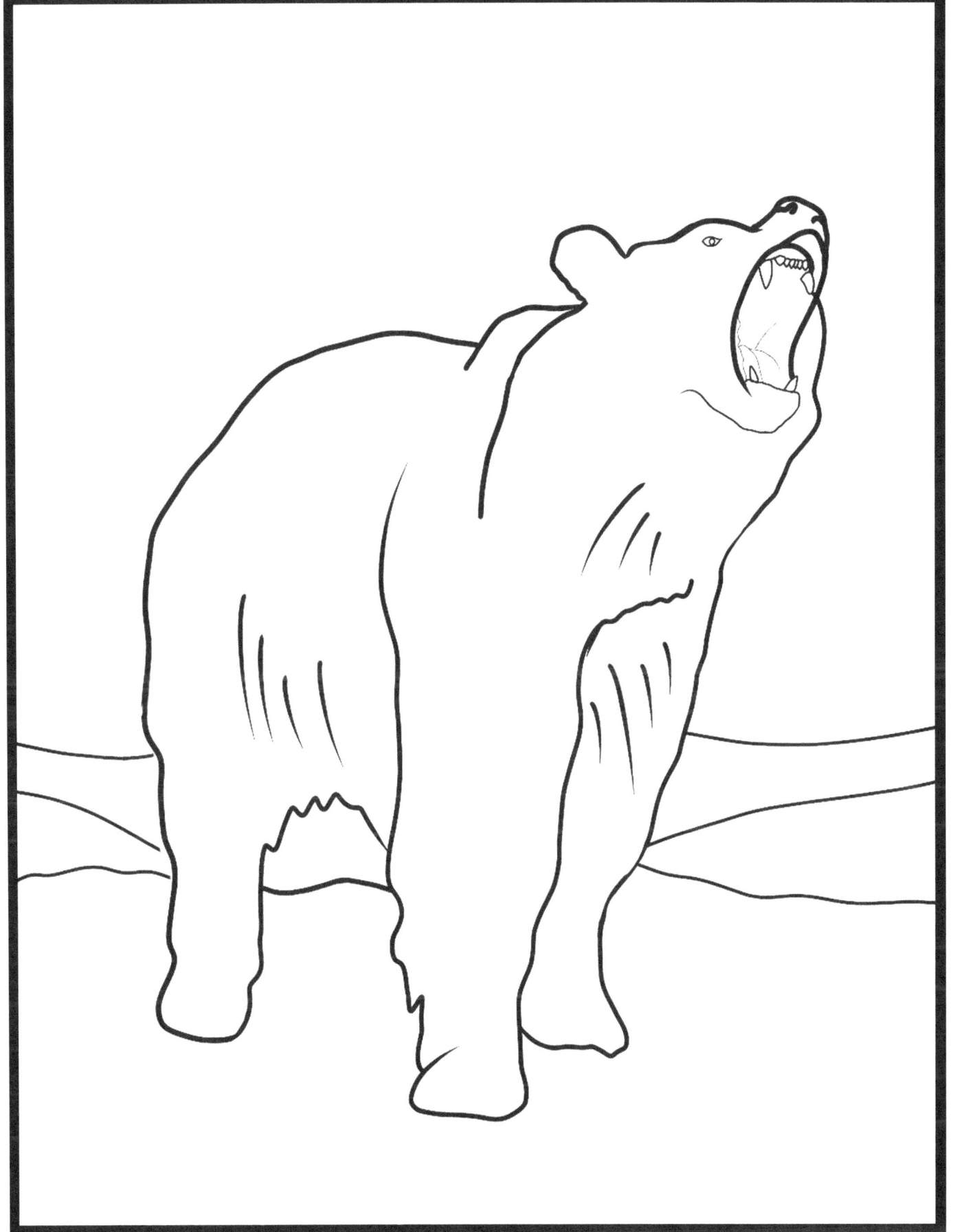

BEAUTIFUL GRIZZLY BEAR

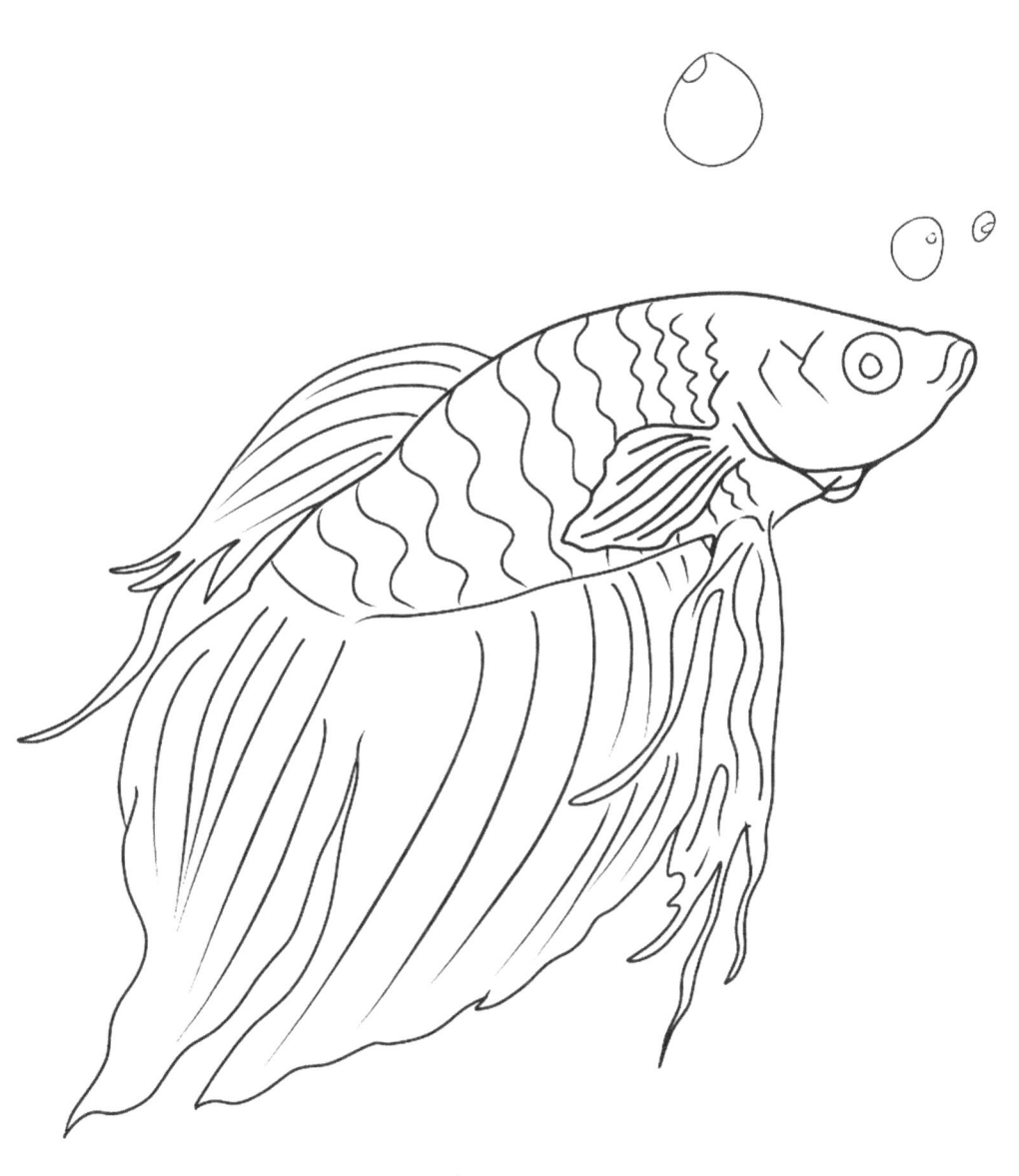

FANTASTIC BETA FISH

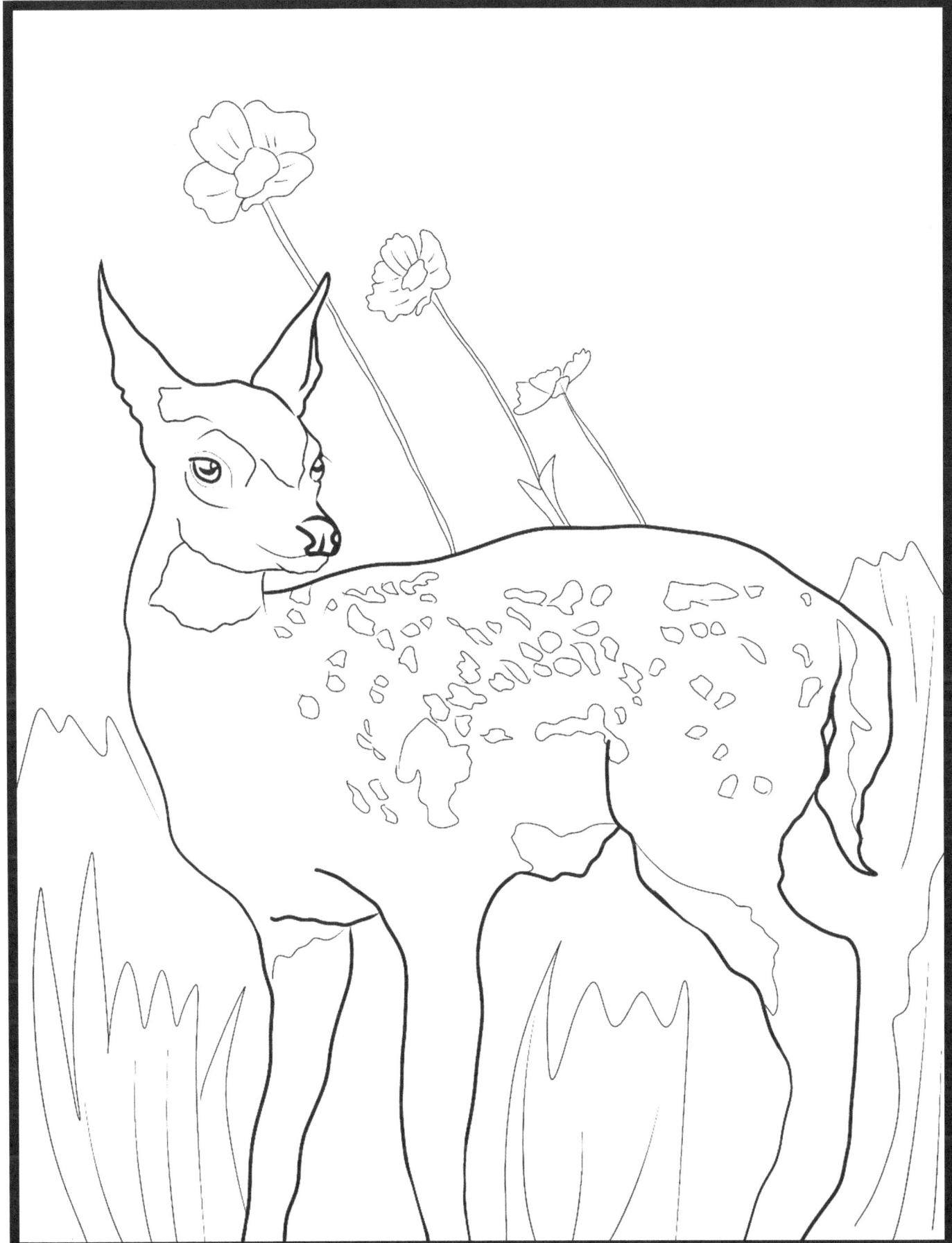

DASHING DEER

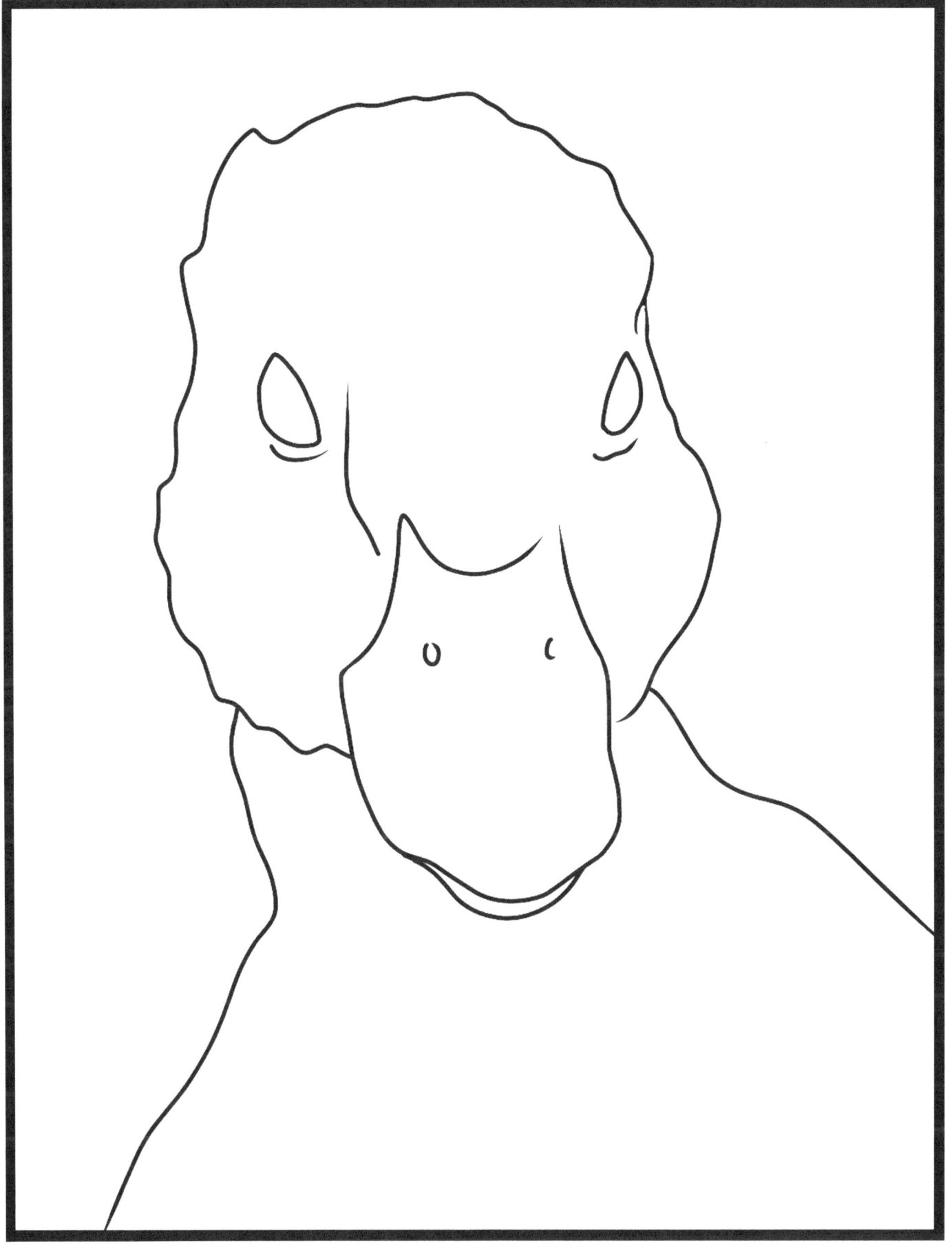

DOWN-TO-EARTH DUCK

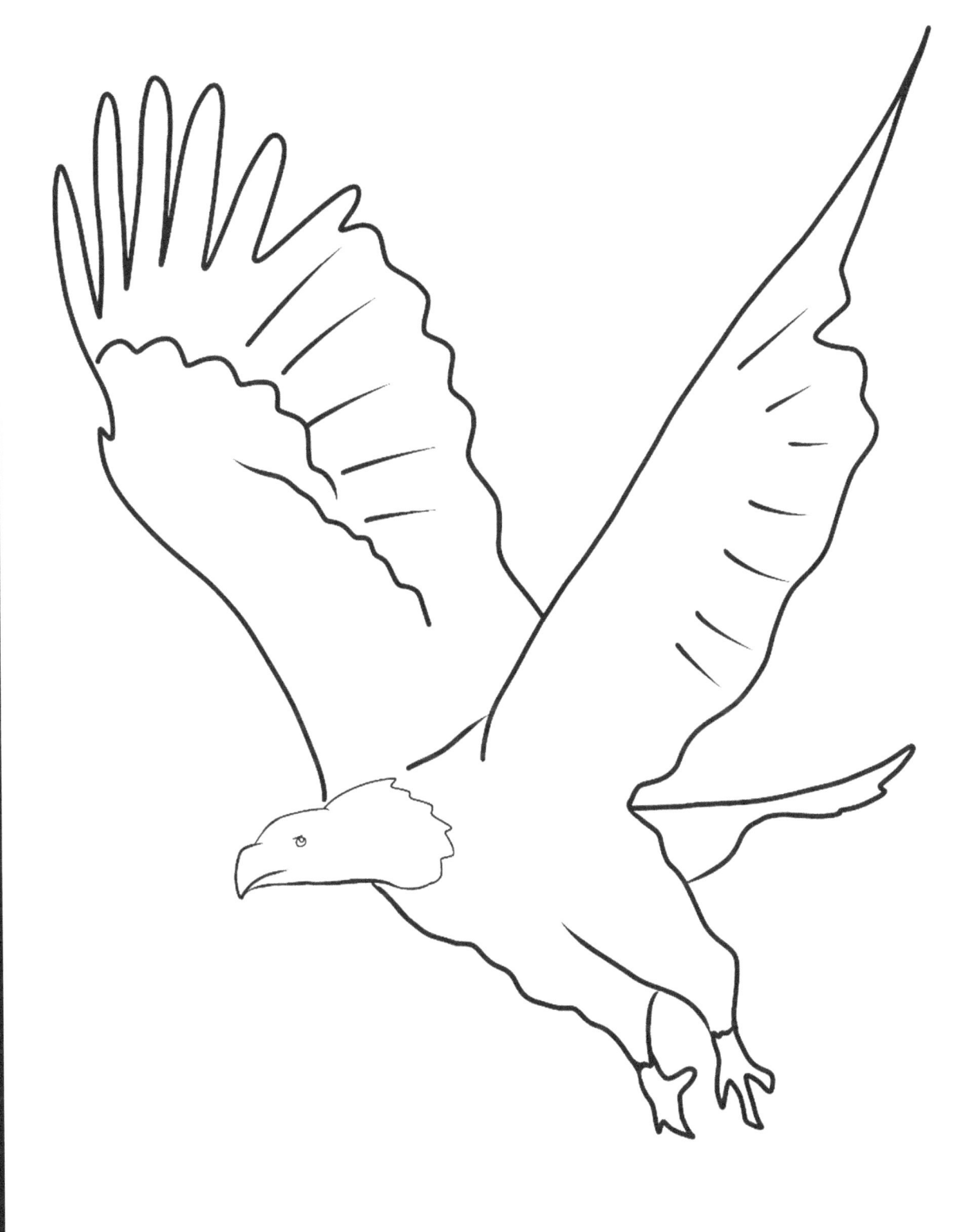

EAGER EAGLE

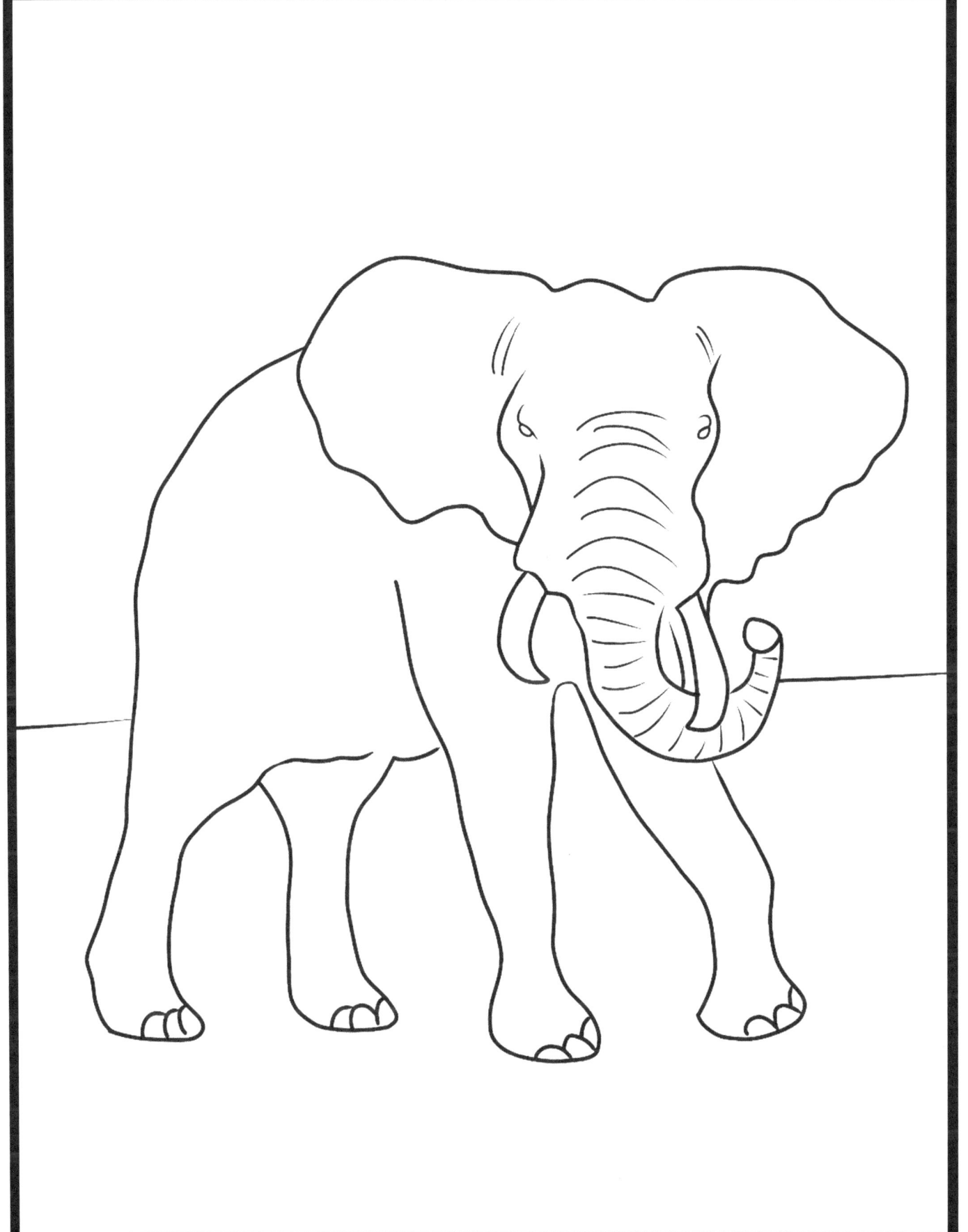

EMPOWERING ELEPHANT

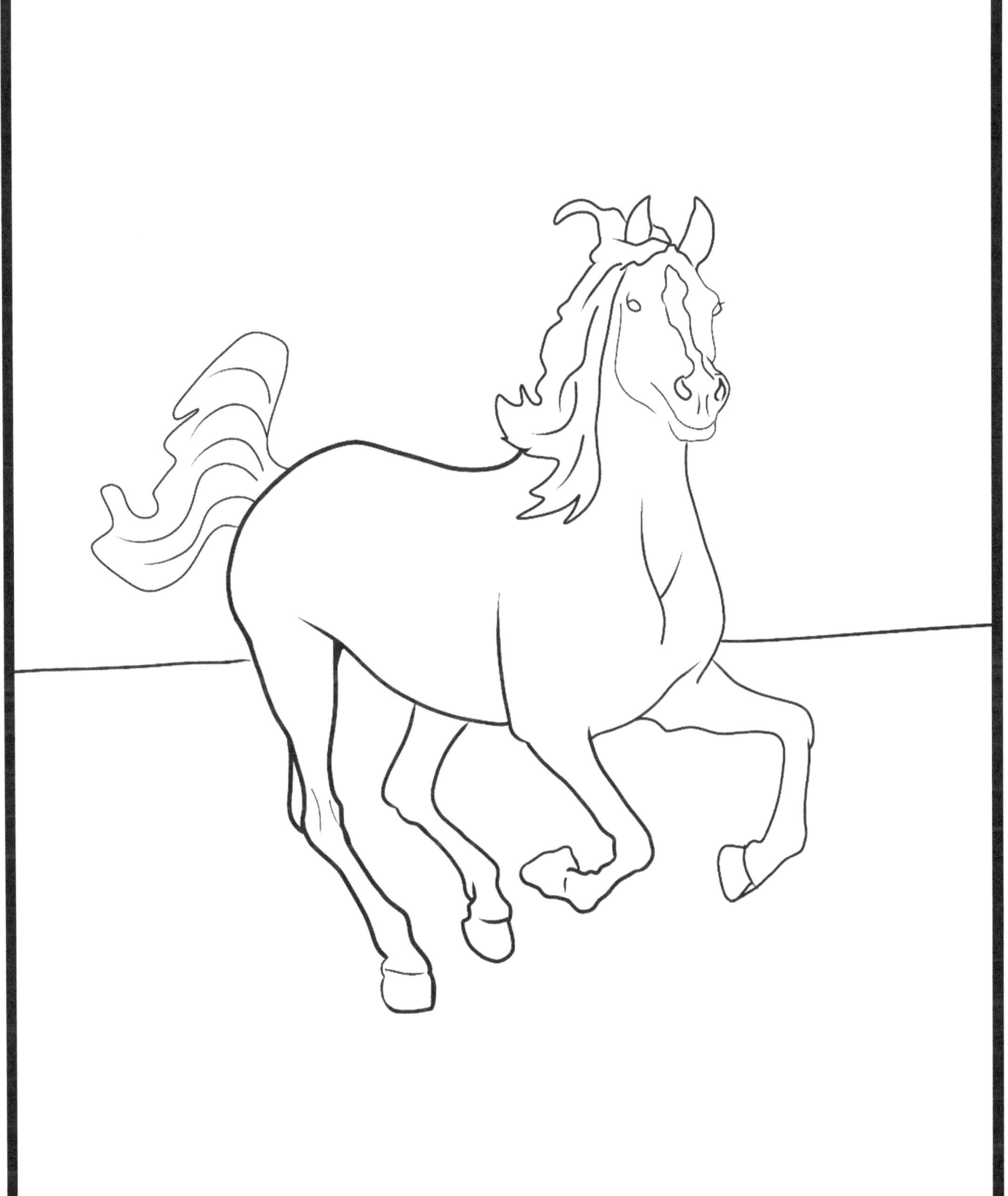

HEARTFELT HORSE

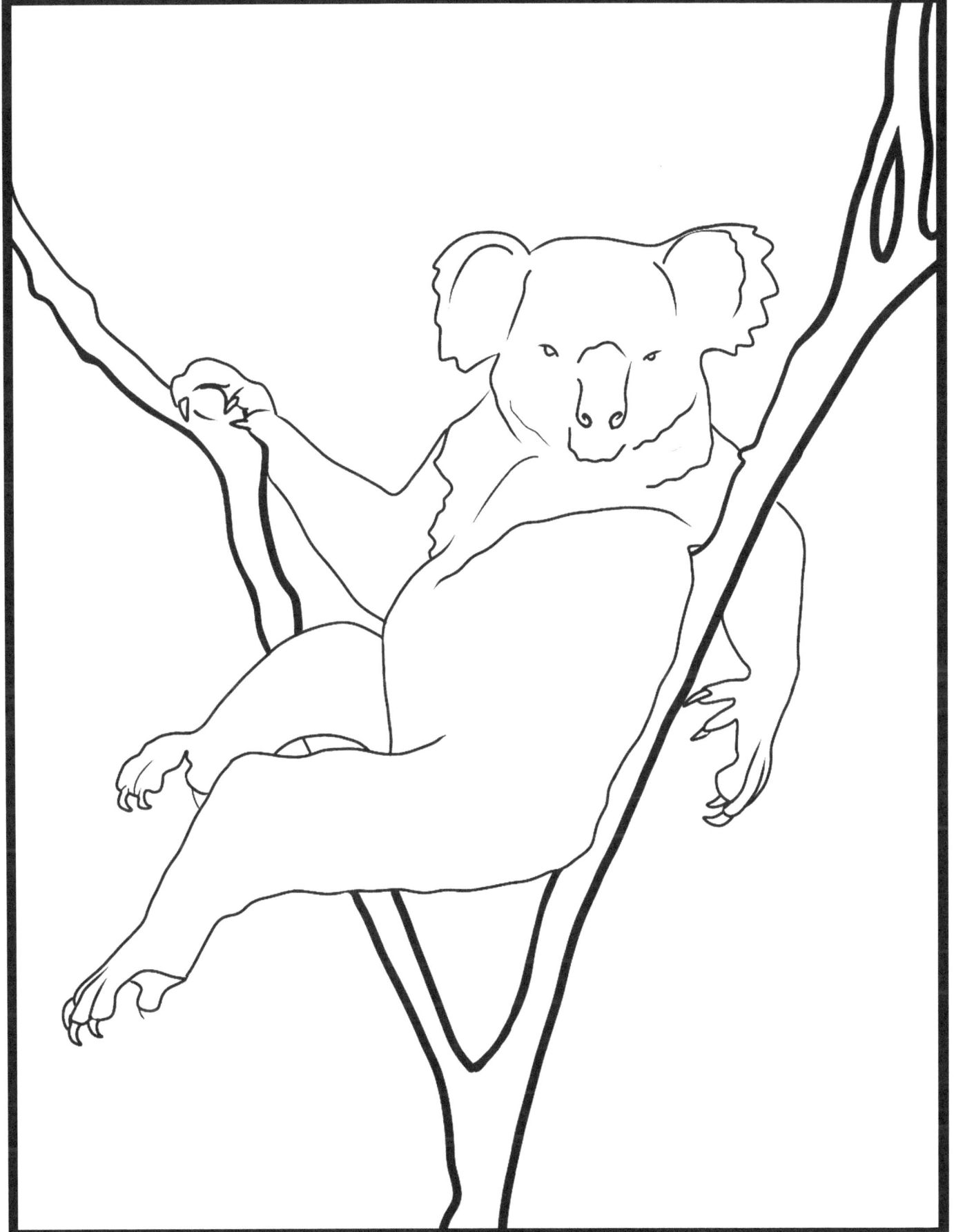

KNOWLEDGABLE KAOLA

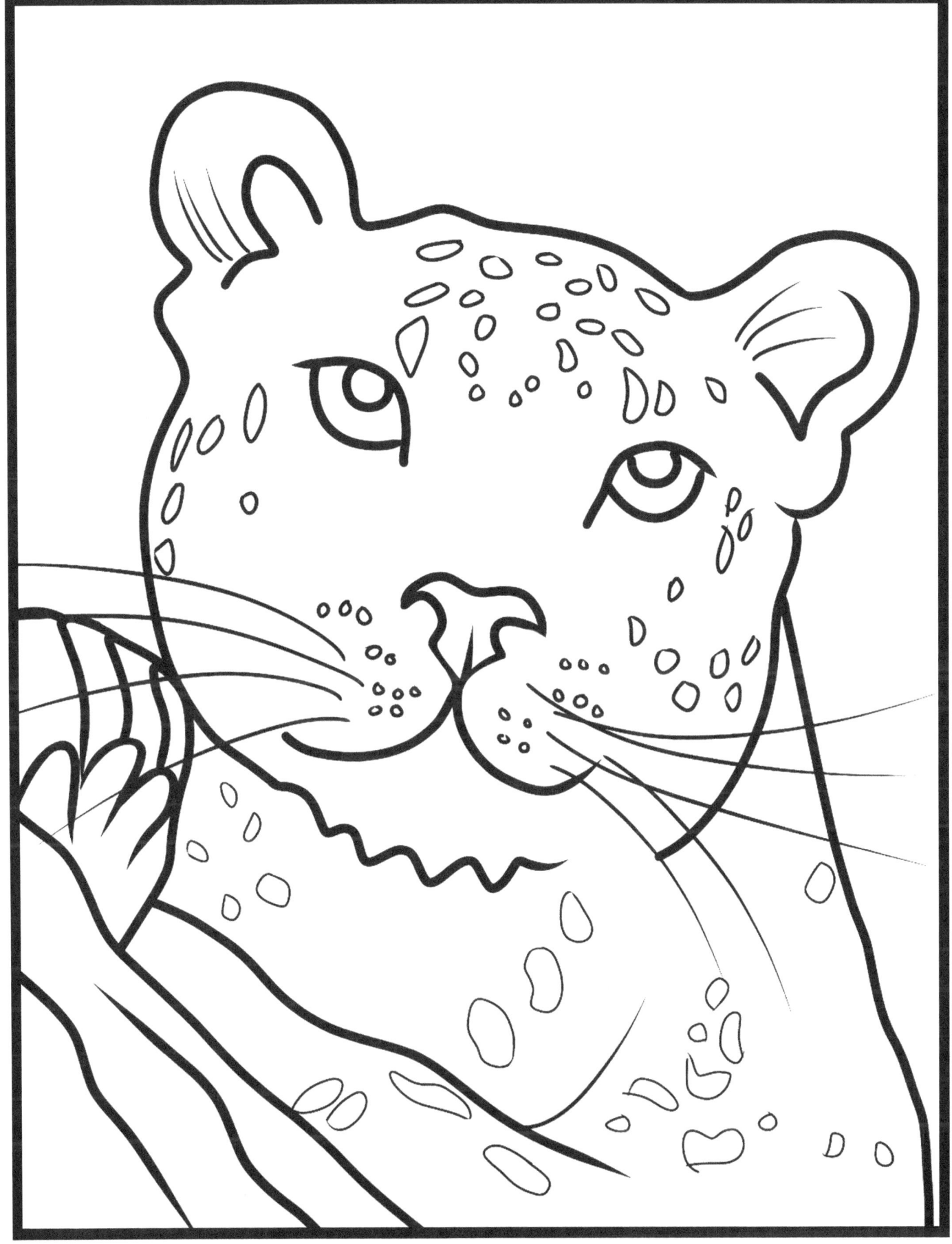

LAID BACK LEOPARD

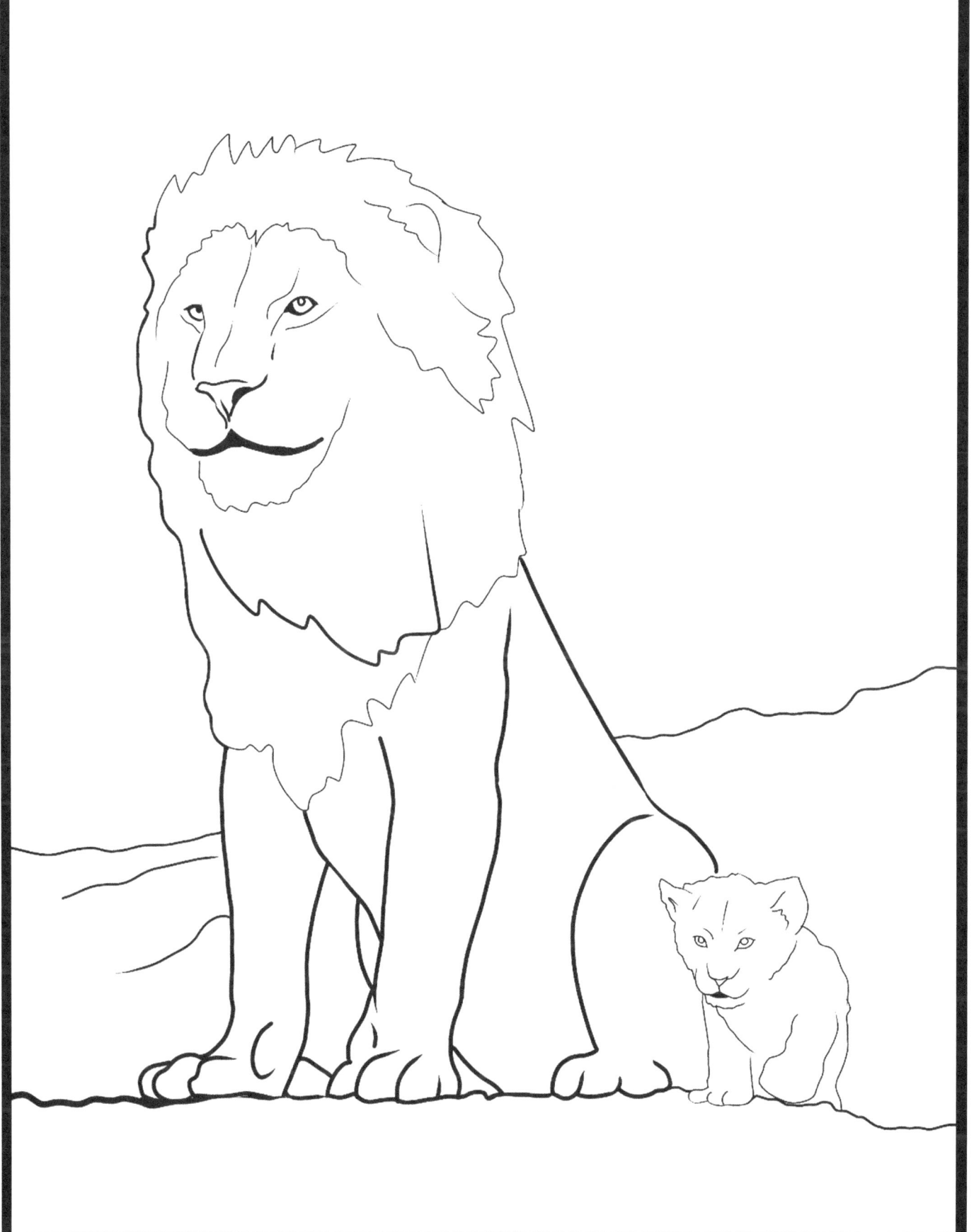

LEGENDARY LION

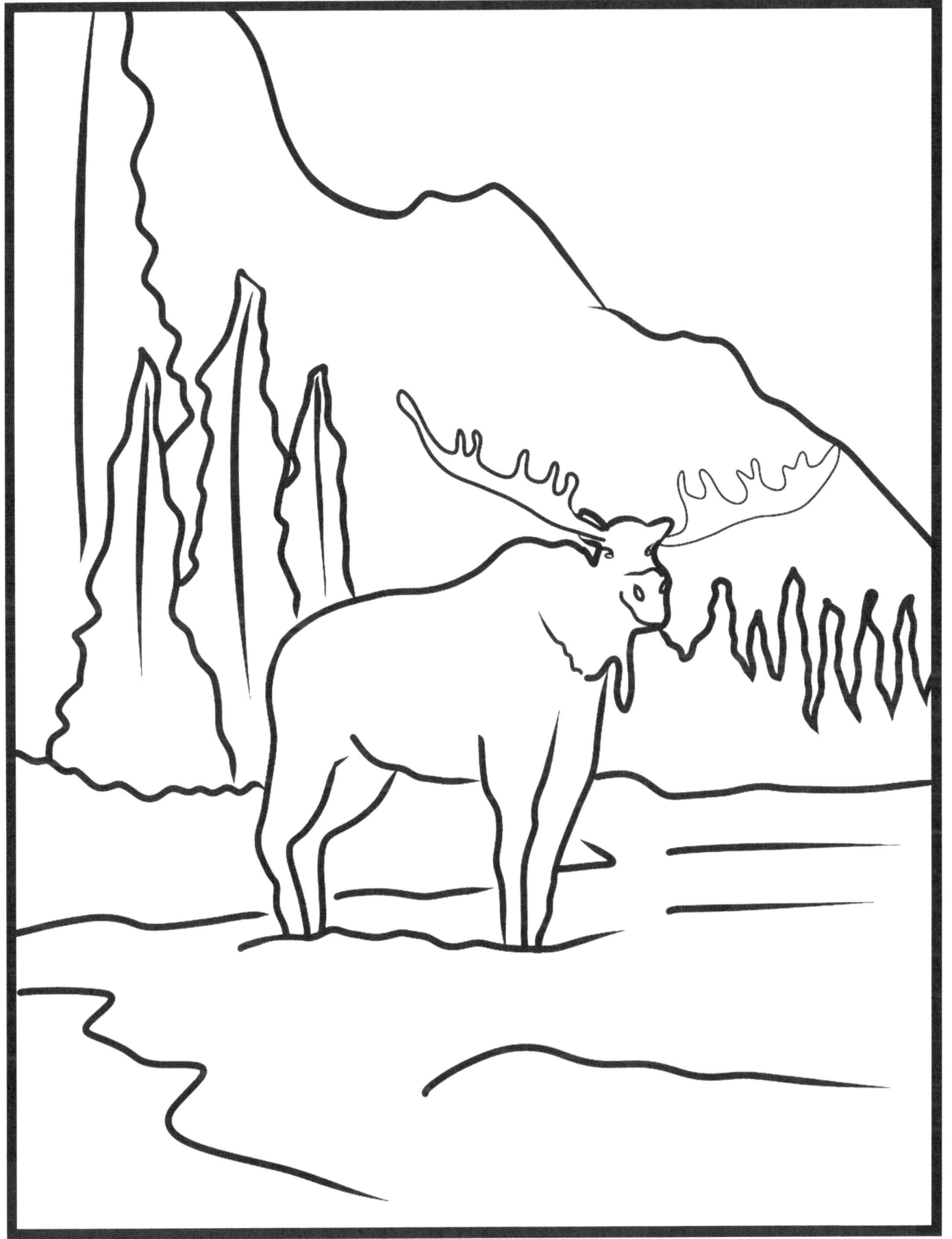

MAGNIFICENT MOOSE

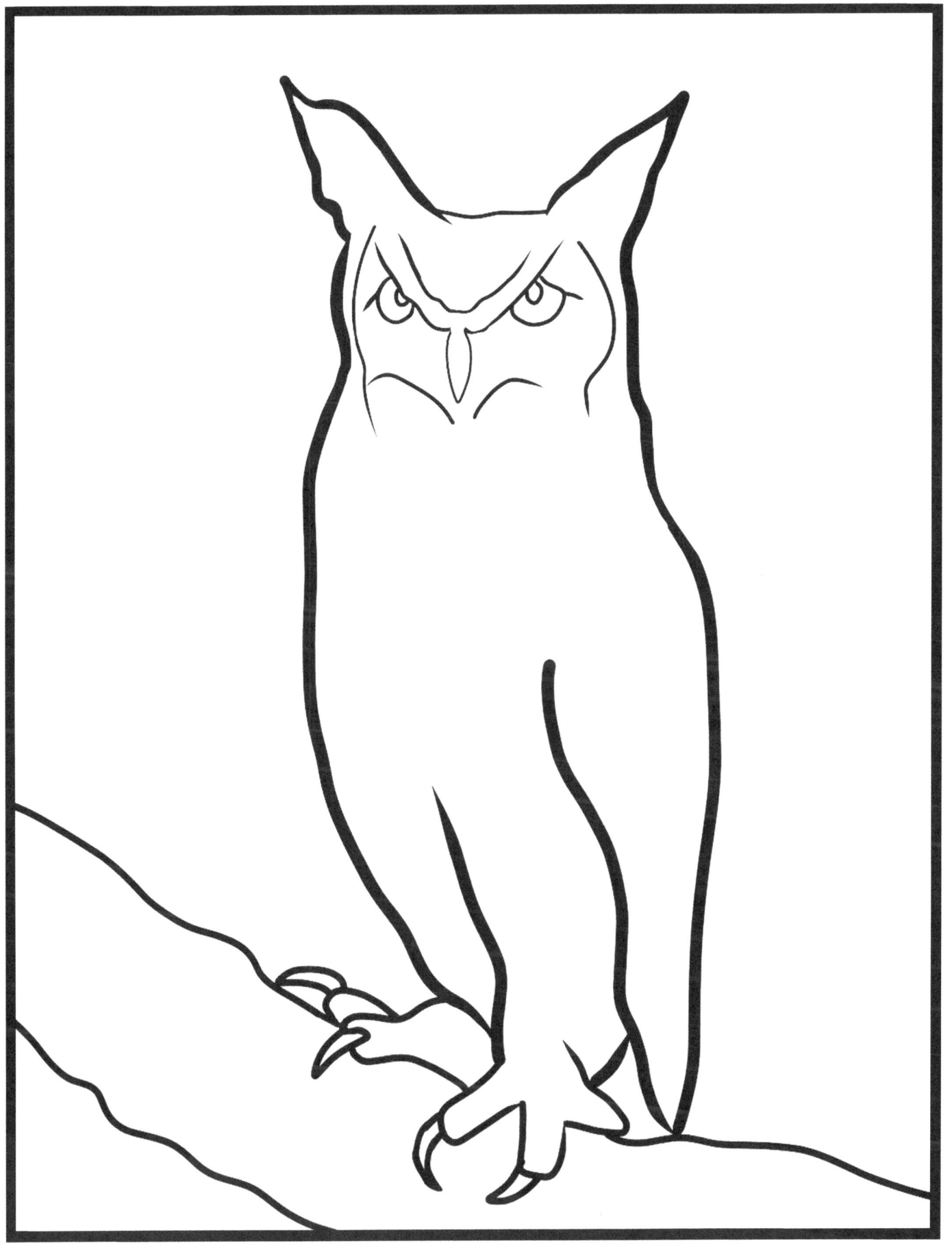

OPTIMISTIC OWL

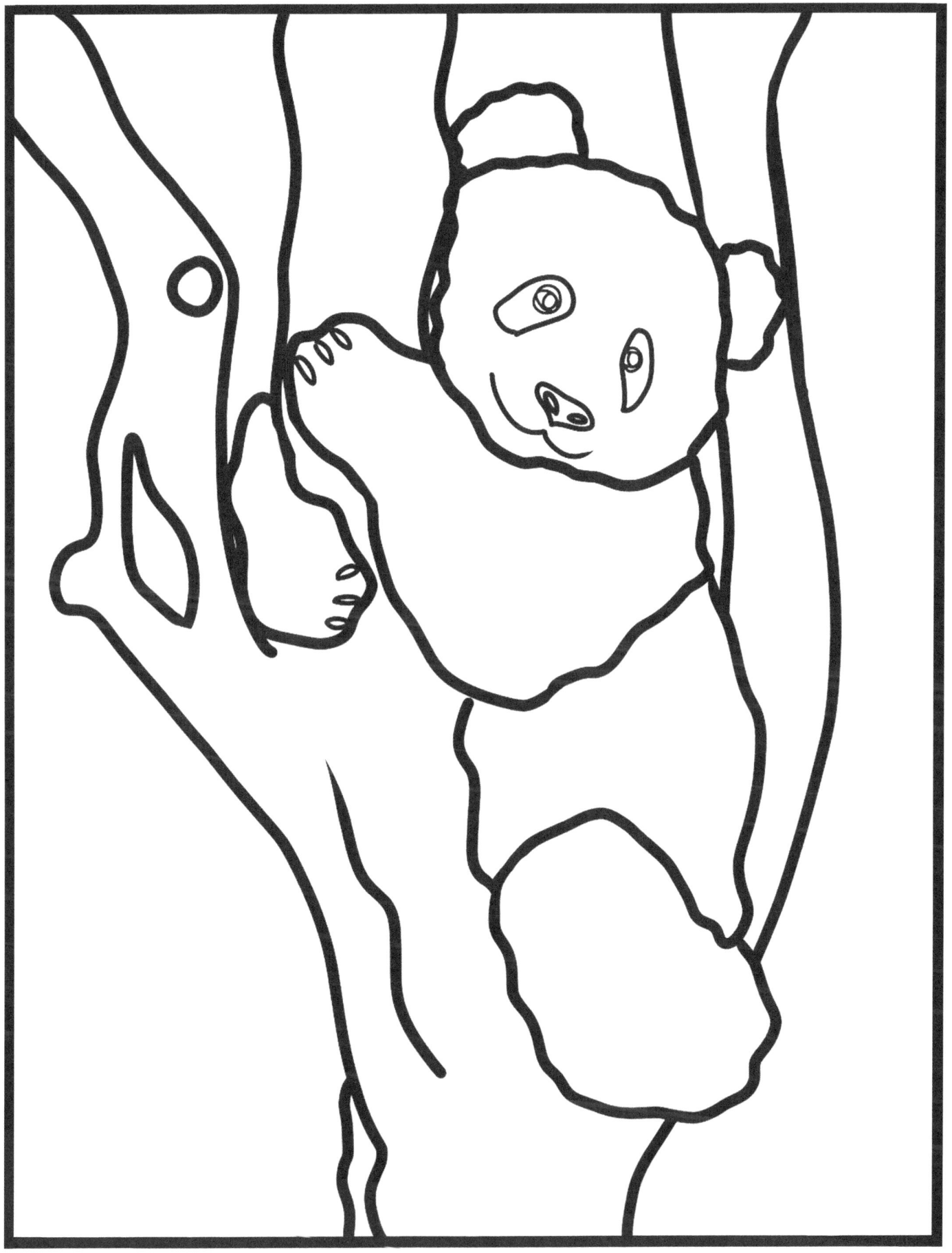

PLAYFUL PANDA

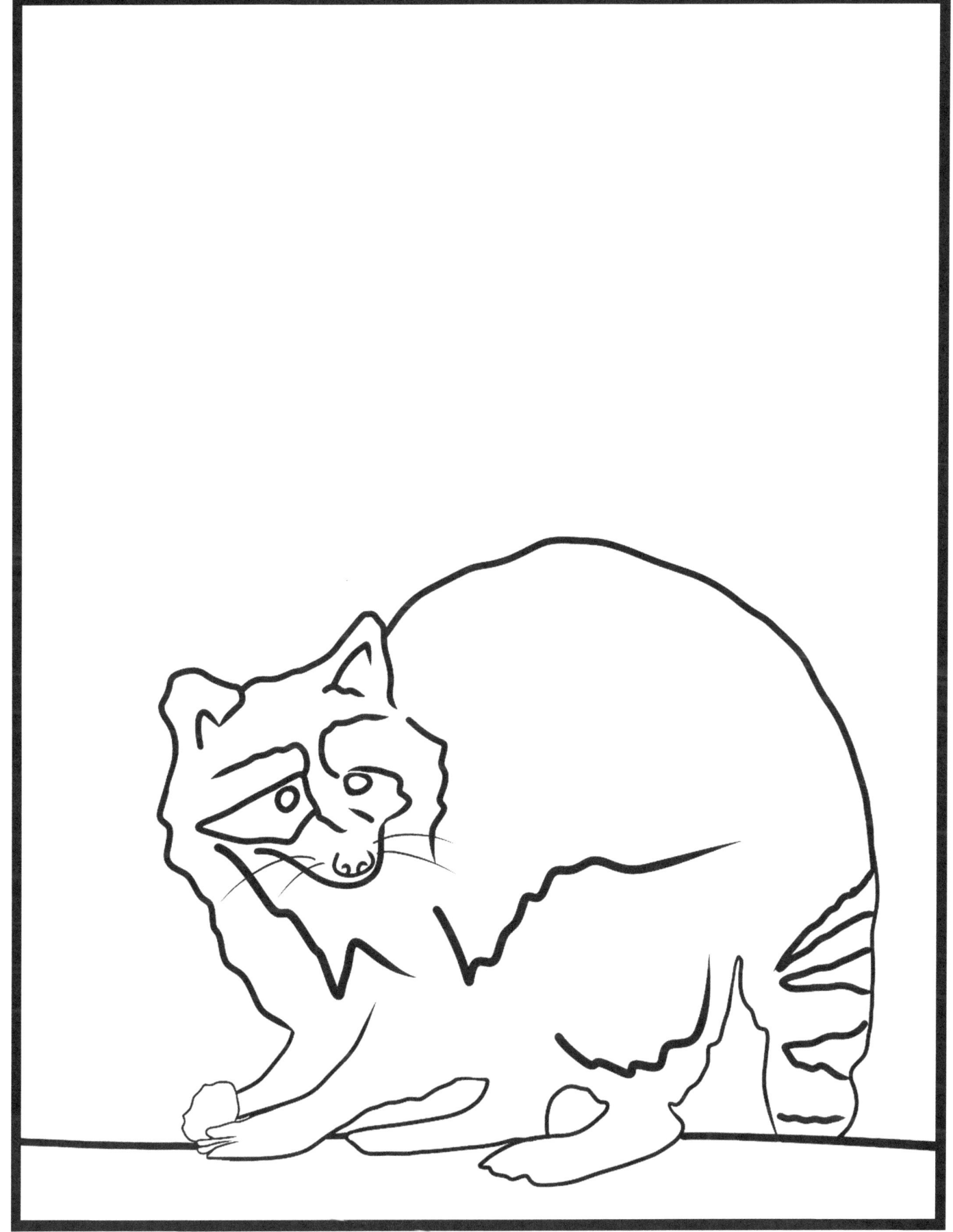

RADIANT RACCOON

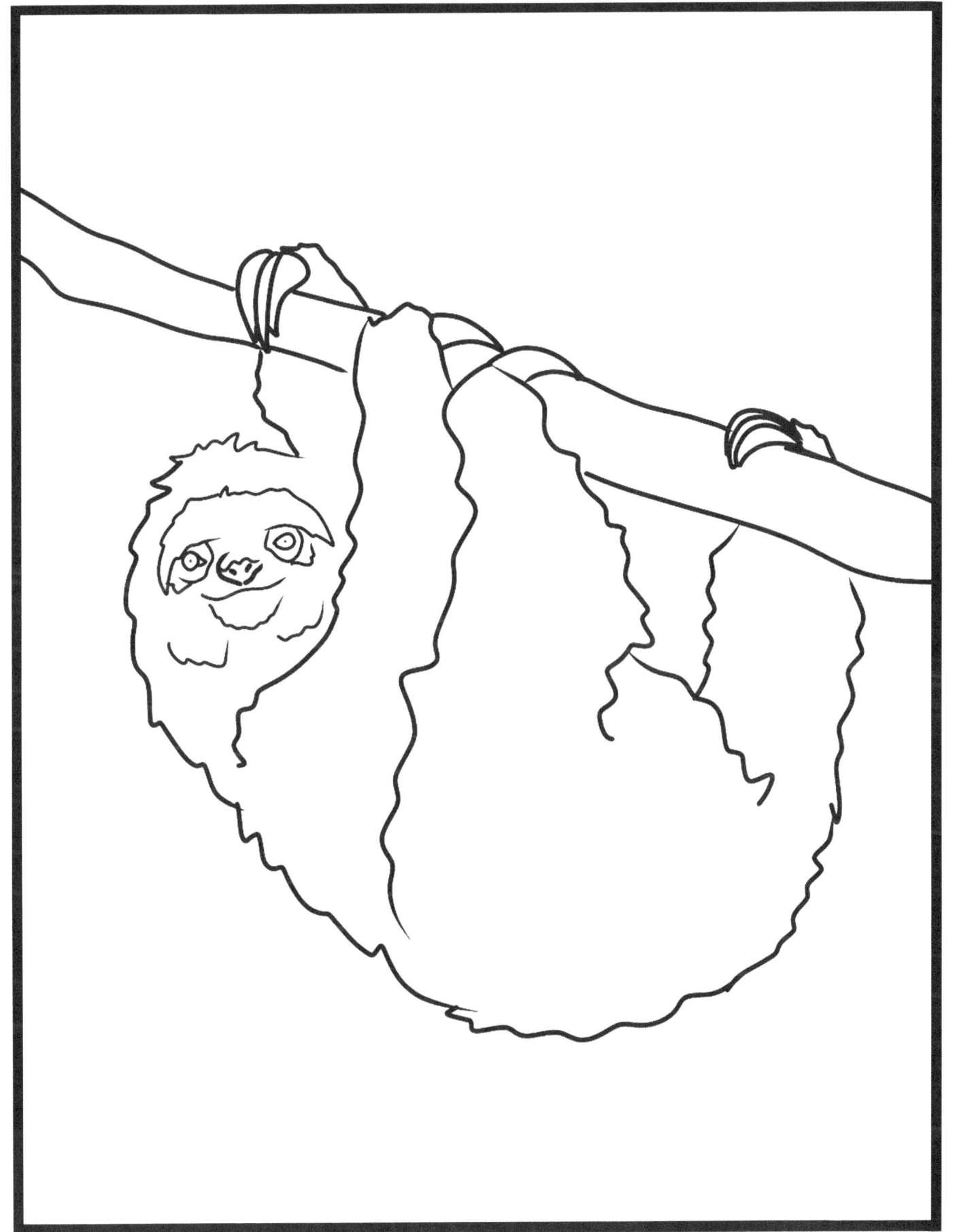

SILLY SLOTH

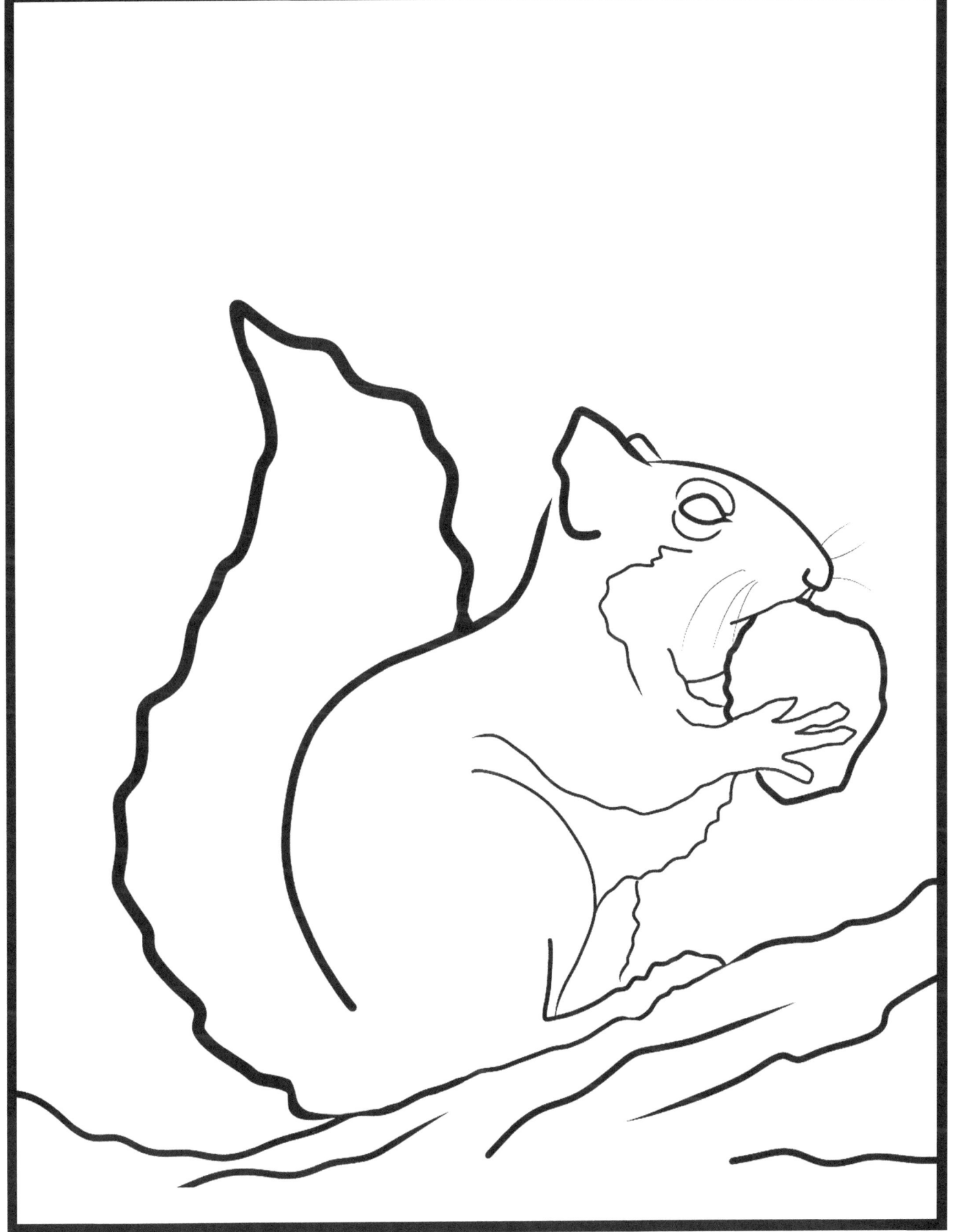

SMART SQUIRREL

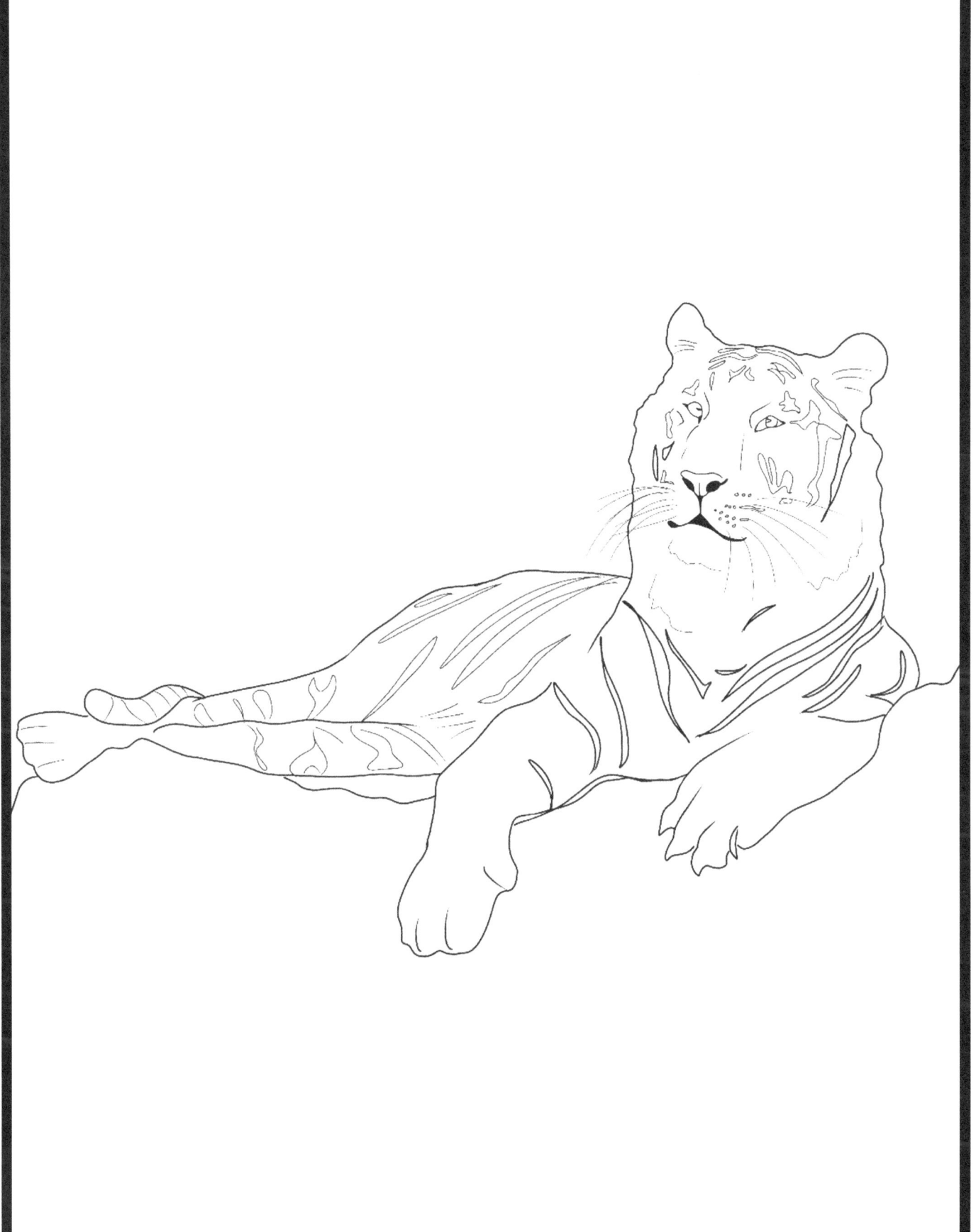

TRANQUIL TIGER

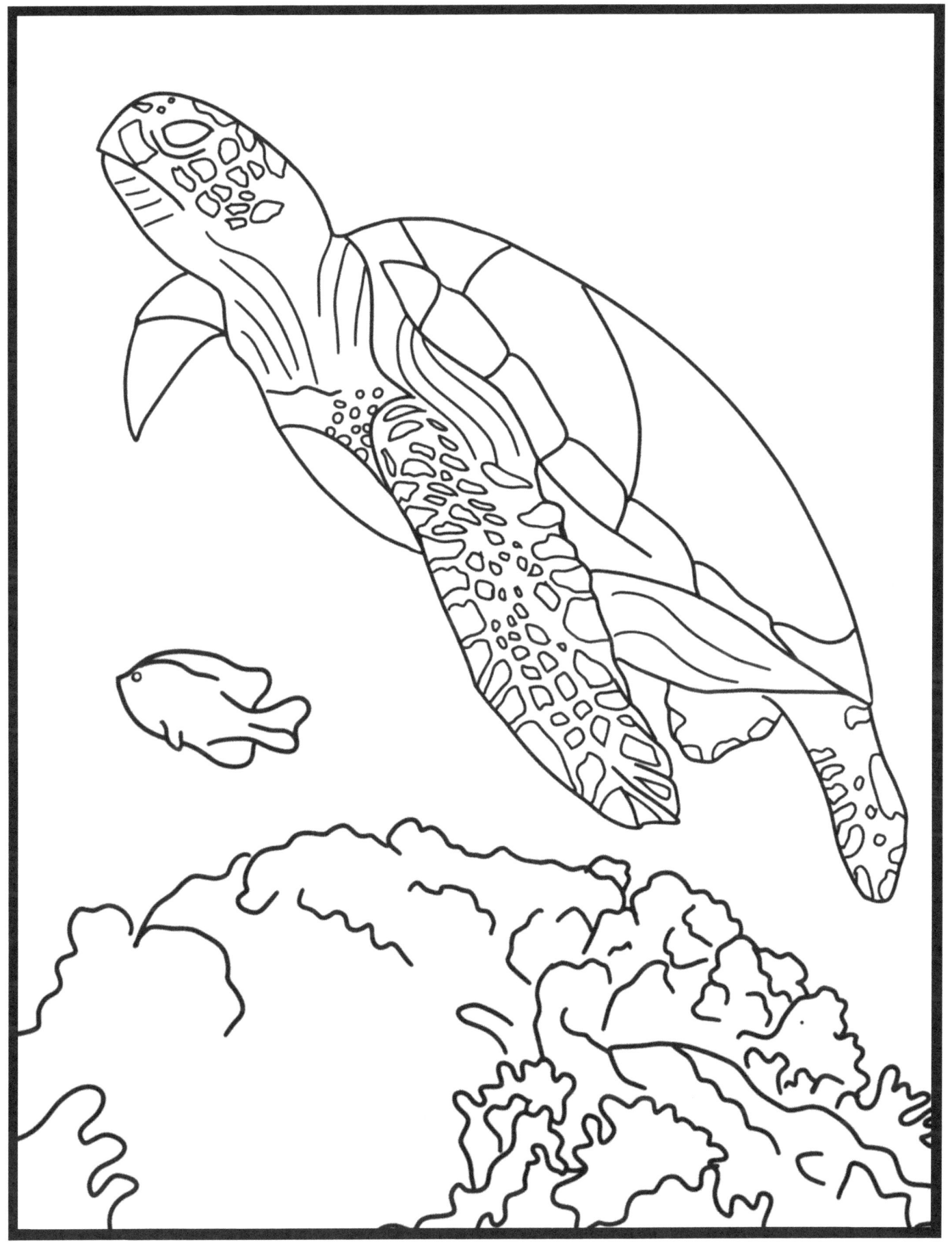

THOUGHTFUL TURTLE

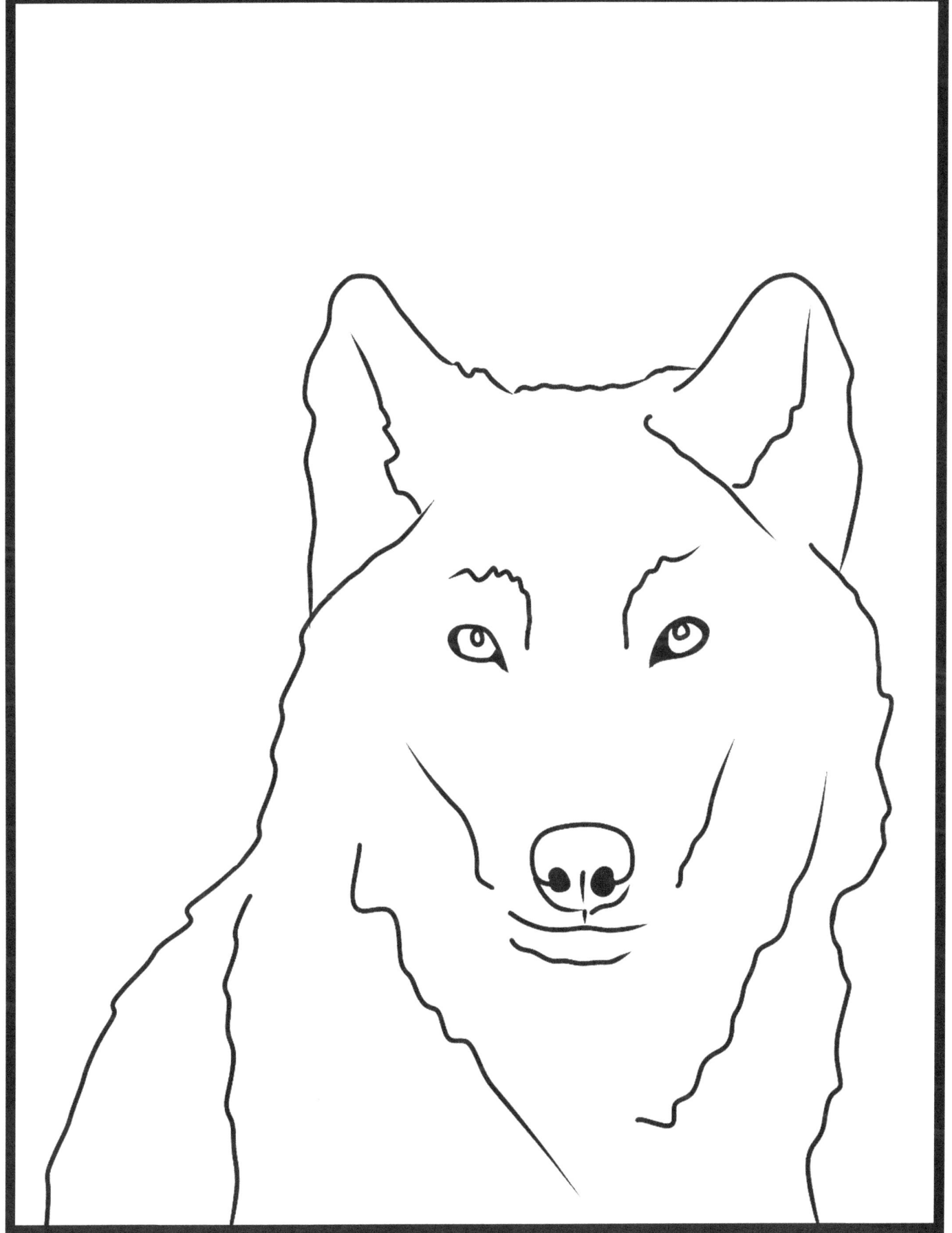

WANDERING WOLF

www.ingramcontent.com/pod-product-compliance
Lightning Source LLC
Chambersburg PA
CBHW081100240526
45465CB00025B/2778